Messages from the Silence

an invitation to the wedding...

Mary Saint-Marie/Sheoekah

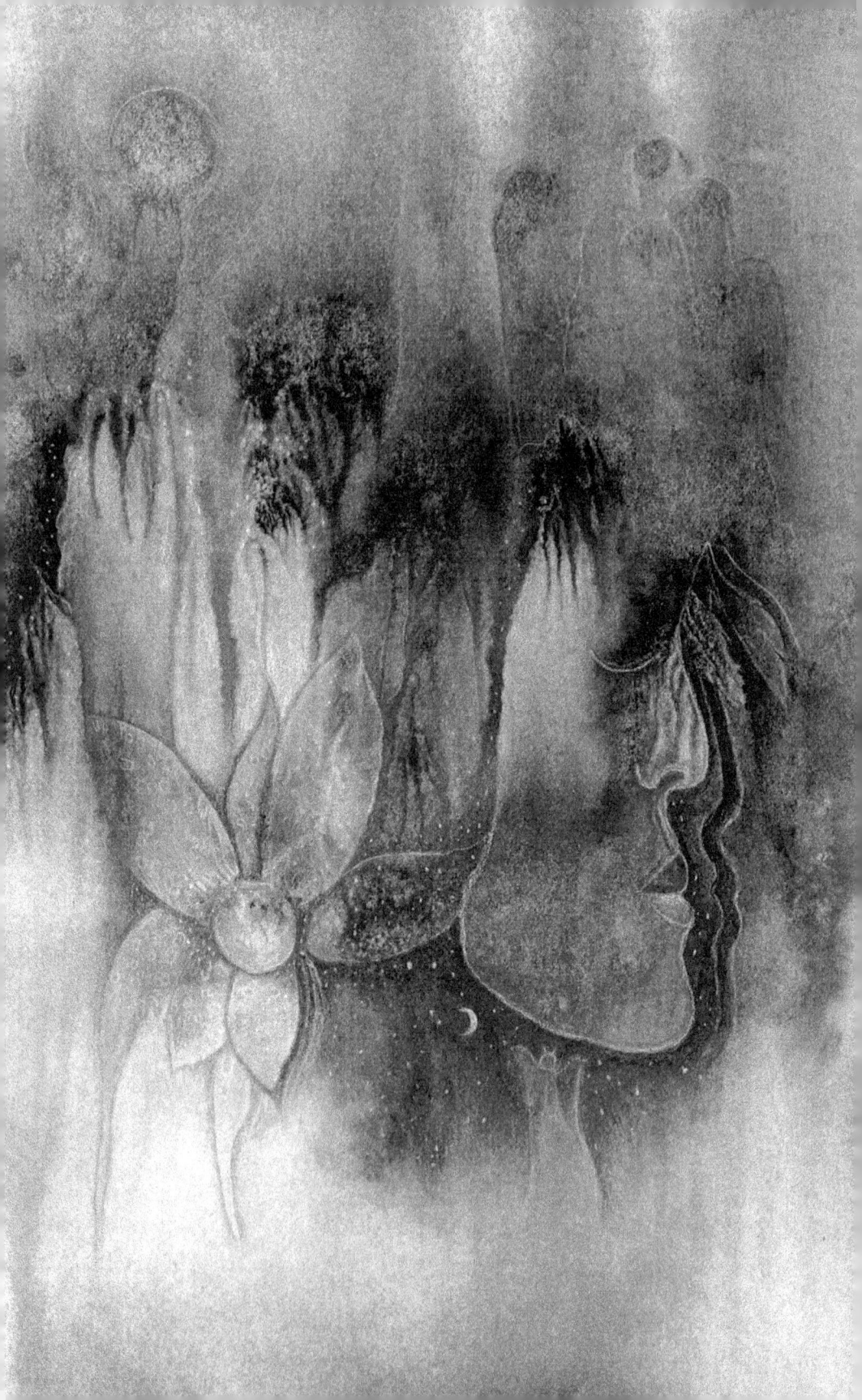

Messages from the Silence

an invitation to the wedding...

Second Edition, Revised 2015
© 2005, 2015 Mary Saint-Marie / Sheoekah. All Rights Reserved.

No part of this book may be reproduced, stored in a retrieval system, or transmitted by any means without the written permission of the author.

Published by Ancient Beauty Studio, www.marysaintmarie.com

ISBN: 978-0-9646572-6-7 (sc)

Photo Credits: Page 127, 130, 133 Kris McMillan

Book Design and Layout by Aaron Rose, Mount Shasta, California

Other publications by Mary Saint-Marie:
Galactic Shamanism
The Holy Sight
Nectar of Woman
The Sacred Two
The Star-Stone Ones
The Animating Presence
The Monitor and Laughter of the Gods
Art As Consciousness
The Oracle and the Dreamer

This book is dedicated to the Silence…

Cover Art and Poem by Mary Saint-Marie

Yellow Flower and SHE

SHE…it is…who heralds…
a new way…
SHE…it is…who prays…
near the flower…
SHE…it is…who remembers…
times gone by…
SHE…heralds the garden…

This image appears to be a mystical landscape. It is calling into memory our oneness with the precious flowers. Out of the Silence… this memory takes flight "into our world." Some would think this imagination and dreamscape…when truly it is Realism seen from a higher altitude. It is the place where reality…essence …is felt. Friends, we must hear and know in this Silence…to create a different world.

*May this book serve to inspire others
to find their own
Messages from the Silence…
in the light of knowing…*

Contents

Acknowledgments 13
Preface 15

Passages in Messages from the Silence

To Surrender 19
Long You Have Asked for Truth 20
The World Is As A Fairy Tale 21
I Am the Question and the Answer 22
By Listening… 23
Nepenthe 24
Voice of Silence 26
And Many Will Say… 30
Dawn Will Come in the Great Embrace 35
The Fragrance of God 39
A Mystery No More 40
Life as Simple 42
The Epiphany Comes… 44
The Giver of Grace 50

Experience with the Plant Kingdom 51

Masquerading Defenses 52

The Stream of Oneness 53

Vision…silent on your tongue… 55

Visitors…in time… 57

Faraway Shores 58

Flowers Speaking from the Silence 59

I Am the Wedding Day 61

Come Child… 62

Friends…you are creation… 63

Inheritance 65

Harmony: Archetypal Goddess of the Ecosystem 66

This Wedding… 68

Abide in Me 70

This River 71

I am the grasses and the grapes… 77

Manes Flying… 84

O Humanity 85

Vessel of the Infinite 87

This Timeless Flow 89

Mystic Marriage 90

The Wordless and Nameless 91

The Holy Presence of Love 93

True Power 95

Got Problems? 97

There Is No Shadow 98

I Desire ONLY Presence: Prayers or Preyers 100

You Have Won the Lottery 106

Experience God 112

The Promise 114

Respond to Inner Vision 116

A Child of Forever 119

Presence Is… 123

True Sustainability 124

Mary Saint-Marie: Artist/Writer 127

Mystic Art, Books, Sessions, and Retreats 131

Acknowledgments

I am in great appreciation for all the ones who have come to me for love in this lifetime. It began with my mother and one of my sisters who were in such pain. Then it was young men. Oh how I did want a normal and stable life with a boyfriend to go steady, during those wild James Dean days. Instead, from ages twelve to seventeen, I dated seventy-five boys. I felt more like a confidante and friend than anything. I visited a chain gang boyfriend in the hospital; another used to have black eyes from time to time from street fights. I was part of the sugar shack, valley girl generation and I seemed to be always just holding space in the Silence. My nickname was Smiley, and I just kept smiling. My life was like none around me as my air force family traveled about in Mississippi, Texas, and Iowa.

I am in great appreciation for all the high school and college level students from my days of teaching. A great many of them were in such emotional turbulence; I realized just loving them was more important than anything I could possibly teach academically.

And in many years of traveling and doing Soul Sessions, retreats, workshops, and art exhibitions, I continue to meet many awake and awakening people. To all of you, I am so grateful. The wonder of sitting in the Silence together and experiencing the energy shift to Love is magnificent. Together we behold the energies borne of separation shift to that of Presence. And lives change.

I thank my precious daughters for all that they went through with a non-conventional mom who was always seeking time to go into the Silence, rather than bake cookies. They heard me say that I need quiet time, as if it were my mantra.

I thank my dear close friends who love me as my life spirals into always new and changing forms and expressions.

I thank you all for the opportunity to sit in the Silence together and know love.

Preface

The Messages from the Silence began to come.

They came on the dawns. They came.

I did not seem to be in control of when they came or on what subject. I would awaken and there would be a strong feeling of the Inner Presence of Spirit along with a phrase or a part of a sentence. I learned to keep light, pen, and paper next to me, so I could just allow the message to come at whatever hour.

The messages came very fast, without my taking any thought. When they came, I was aware also of the message, as an awareness, on an expanded non-verbal level. It is not easy to describe, but it is a pervasive awareness and field of direct knowing. It is an expanded and exalted feeling. Luminous. The mind feels free on a new level of being.

These messages from the Inner Silence began to come while I was on retreat in Crestone, Colorado during the winter of 1997 and 1998. They continued when I began a writing sabbatical in Arizona. The messages no longer came just in the dawns and pre-dawns. Sometimes they came when I was driving on a road or even a freeway. I learned to take paper and pen with me everywhere. When a realization came in the form of a message, I needed to be prepared.

It was during the retreat in Arizona that I became aware that these realizations were to be shared in a book called *Messages from the Silence*. The messages continued randomly until early 2005 when I became aware that it was time to publish them.

I offer them now as inspirations and catalysts to others to find "direct knowing" from within…

Note about the writing style:

Because these writings are stream-of-consciousness, italics have been used at times to denote subtle shifts within a passage. Sometimes the "messages" speak from a "we" perspective and other times the messages shift to an intimate communion of speaking directly to a "you." Other times the shift is into the illumined first person of Presence, the Impersonal and holy I.

Reading the messages aloud emphasizes that shift, as the messages come with an intonation of strong intent. Even gathering as The People of the Circle and having a person read a passage aloud powerfully accentuates the messages and allows the inflow of Presence. The messages are as passages from one state of consciousness to another…and those passages may be felt.

Passages in Messages from the Silence

To Surrender

To surrender, go into the Silence with no desire, save one.
To be One with me.

To move forth into your day in surrender,
maintain your consciousness of Oneness with me.

Be in judgment of no one…for any reason.
Allow each person to act out their beliefs.
When it is time, they too,
one at a time,
will come with bended knees,
in surrender when their life fails
and their world of illusion falls apart.
Then comes their Moment…
to come unto me…
the Father…
and Be at One…

Child, yes, come in surrender.
The way will be shown.

August 29, 1998 in Sedona, Arizona

Long You Have Asked for Truth

It is I...child.
I have come to take you home.

It is I...child.
It is I that arrives in the personal surrender.

Long you have asked for Truth.

You have asked to know the Truth no matter what the consequences. You have watched lies and deception and wrong relationships be exposed...just by calling deeply for the Truth.

Long ago you read in many different Teachings...know the Truth and the Truth will set you free. So you have set that in motion.

Call only for the Truth to be revealed and that which is not the Truth to be exposed. Little do the masses realize what power is in the desire to know the Truth.

The Truth, my child, is My Kingdom.
That is "my kingdom come" in the consciousness of all who ask.

The Truth will change the world as you currently know it.

Continue to call for the Truth.

August 31, 1998 in Sedona, Arizona

The World Is As A Fairy Tale

The world is as a true fairy tale.
And as in many fairy tales,
there has been a curse or a spell.

The world, humanity, just like the fairy tales, is under a spell. The spell is the sense of separation. The spell is…the cloak of forgetfulness…that comes when we humans left the kingdom, the consciousness of the heaven world, the unity, the union, God.

From that moment we have lived in separation, which is fear and pain. It is the concepts of good and evil…everyone disagreeing with each other.

How do we break this spell? Did all the great teachers…Krishna, Buddha, Lao Tzu, Jesus, and others…break the spell for their own lives?

Why is it that more have not found the way to break the spell… and to enter the kingdom…and…as in the fairy tales…live happily ever after?

Desire to enter the Kingdom is the first step
in this pilgrimage to the Holy of Holies
that is without place or time.

October 22, 1998 in Sedona, Arizona

I Am the Question and the Answer

I am the question and the answer.
If you stay attuned to me,
the impersonal I within,
I will give you revelations.
I will give you revelations that just flow through,
no questions asked.
Questions and answers still need separation.
In the attunement, there will only be knowing,
direct knowing.

January 11, 1999 in Sedona, Arizona

By Listening...

Humanity makes a mistake.
It wants to talk to me.
What is needed is that humanity listen.

It is I who will talk.
It is humanity who listens.
It is in listening in the Silence
that humanity knows what to do.

By listening in the invisible world,
humanity comes to know what to do
in the visible world.

By listening in the unformed world,
one comes to know what to do
in the formed world.

By listening in the wordless world,
one knows what to say
in the world full of words.

By listening in the timeless world,
one knows how to show up in time.

This world of Silence,
wherein messages flow,
is a world of paradox.

January 16, 1999 in Arizona

Nepenthe

In this Silence, does dwell an ecstasy, a rapture.
Perhaps this Silence is the Nepenthe the Greeks did look for,
a drug to forget all sorrows.

My friends, Silence is that substance, that drink,
in which we forget all sorrows.
Drink of this Silence.
It is the elixir of the Holy Grail.
It is the answer…before the question.
It is the solution…before the problem.

Humanity chooses to stay in charge,
chooses to use free will.
Humanity chooses the course of its own downfall,
its own destruction.

Messages from the Silence, through all humanity, can change all that. Many are…this day…changing all that. Each individual can ride on the crest of this incoming Consciousness from the Silence. It is purely a matter of choice.

Western World wants the human rightness and wrongness.
It loves to battle in the polarities.
It loves to battle.
My friends, this battle, I tell you, it is a choice.
Battles are a choice at whatever level they occur.

Battles or Grace.
It seems an easy choice, does it not?
Who would choose battles when Grace is possible?
Humanity would do that.

One person by one person,
humanity will turn to Grace.
One person by one person,
humanity will choose the Silence.

Messages from the Silence will create a new world.

Each person shall speak, move, act
from that place in the Silence.

One person by one person
a new world shall spring forth.
Each one person shall touch all in their lives.

Each life will be a beacon.
Each life will be a clarion call.
Each life will be a flower of the Infinite.

And the garden…it will be again…

It is here now. The Garden. Nepenthe.
It is that humanity must take notice.

January 16, 1999 in Arizona

Voice of Silence

I Am the only Presence here.
In that recognition…in that acknowledgment…
what is your day and what is your night?
Imagine. I Am the only Presence here.

As you drive your car to work…to play…
as you walk, bike, ski, and on…
what now are the differences…
in what you think and do…
and what you see?

I am the only Presence here.
New choices to be made.
Vast great changes.
They are happening even now.

I am the only Presence here.
I am in the birds. I am the birds.
I am in the sky. I am the sky.
I am in the earth. I am the earth.
I am Present in all the kingdoms.
I am Present in the elements.

What choices will you make?
I am Everywhere.
How does that change the day?
How does that change the night?

My friends…
Look out about you and see that I am everywhere.
Look out around you and know that I am everywhere.

Experience my Presence everywhere.

It is clear now why there is human resistance to "messages from the silence." The changes that are to be made in the transition from human consciousness to My Consciousness are vast.

Humanity still fears change, rather than seeing it as life's adventure. Humanity tries to stop the flow of life for the sake of security, as fear is in charge, wherever "messages from the silence" are not heard.

Humanity. Harken. Harken now.
This is that moment.
It is the moment we have all waited for.

All these eons have been a journey
to finally come to the moment to experience Oneness,
Oneness with me, Creator.
That Oneness is also with Creation.
With all Creation.

Here we are. At the brink of Oneness.
Separation or Oneness. That is the choice.
That has always been the choice.

Some of you are frightened to listen to the *Voice of Silence.* You might not hear it right. "Better play it safe and figure things out with the human mind. My mind will keep me safe."

Others of you are frightened of the *Voice of Silence,* as well. But you are frightened for different reasons.

You are fearful that your desires will be thwarted.
You are fearful that your desires will go unfulfilled.

So you reason that you had better stick tight to the logic of the mind. It will get you all the things you want. Then you will be fulfilled.

Others of you are frightened of the *Voice of Silence,* because you fear it will be a voice from regions of evil or from voices on the astral plane. You fear being possessed. It is an area humanity at large is not ready to openly address.

Even that fear, my friends, is not one that can continue. Each person must learn to go into the Silence within. The capital on the word Silence has a very important purpose.

> The Silence indicates My Silence.
> The Silence of God.
> I am that Silence.

To close one's eyes and travel out into nether regions is not wise. It gives power to the mental miscreations of humanity. We need not give power to lies, by going there, by putting our intent and attention there. Should we join into that adventure of miscreation, we have asked for it. Would we walk needlessly into any form of warring zone?

We are called on now to open our consciousness to the *Voice of Silence* from our own inner Silence that calls. We do that by the experience of "I and God are One." It is that Oneness that is the safe place. It is our Consciousness.

> One by one humanity left that Oneness Consciousness.
> One by one humanity returns.
> One by one humanity is taking the responsibility
> to Return to the One.
> One by one humanity takes it upon itself
> to enter the Oneness experience.

That purity of desire will lead humanity to the "how"…to experience the Oneness. Each one shall find the way.

I Am the Way.
What does this mean?
I Am the Way.

I am the only Presence Here.
I am Everywhere.
I am already Here.

I am is God.

Wow. Humanity has a shift to make.
It will make it.
It is making it.
It is happening now.

It matters not where you are in the journey.
Joyfully begin where you are.

Humanity is the prodigal son.
And it…is on its journey home.

I welcome you.
I have been waiting.
I have been knocking.

As One, we have an adventure ahead.
Let us, one by one, begin.

January 16, 1999 in Arizona

And Many Will Say...

Many will want to say
they are finally gaining their power.

*Dear ones...
there is no power to gain.
You already are. That power is within.*

Those who think they are gaining power or have personal power are preparing for a fall. A great fall.

Only the personality believes it has power. The Soul...it is... who knows there is but One Power and it is the Power of God. And it cannot be used. Quite the contrary, It has come to "use" us, the vessel, the hollow reed, the temple template of Infinity. It is the instrument that is used, not the power. Humanity has it backwards, in reverse.

Spirit uses our mind, our voice, our heart, our body...to live its Life.

*Humanity is the vehicle through which I live,
through which I move,
through which I have my Being.
I am the Power.*

*One by one, each person must come unto Me, the One,
with open heart, open mind...
to receive the substance of Light.
To receive my messages from the Silence.*

I Am come to live Life through you.
I Am come to play through you.
I Am come to enjoy through you.
And to love through you.
I Am come to delight in Earth's treasures through you.
And to greet the morning sun…
and the evening star…

I Am come…
I Am Nepenthe…
that which causes forgetfulness of all sorrows…
I Am that drink,
that elixir for which you do search…
And I dwell ever in your Consciousness.
I await your coming.

And many will say to you
that they always invoke the ancestors
before they pray or meditate.
And yet they sit in such wonder
of what is wrong in their world.

Dear ones…many of your ancestors were greatly unillumined. In fact, many lived the deepest portion of their lives…lost in separation from Me. Their lives became one of quiet anguish and quiet desperation…a life of no avail.

You call in these dead ancestors, who hang earthbound, because of their consciousness and their desires, at your own risk. The world you enter in with them is your own co-creation. But do not think you are hearing God, hearing messages from the silence, when they do speak in cryptic tongue.

And do not ask, what has happened, when these ancestors do begin to live your lives. Do not wonder why.

Humanity then would ask…"Who would we invoke?" Invoke the illumined ones. Invoke their holy presence as you begin to make your passage of consciousness back to the One, to Me, to God, to the wordless and the nameless, though names many do you give to me.

My name is I…
and I am everywhere, in everyone and in everything.

Does that not give all a clue
of how to perceive your surroundings, your environment,
all the kingdoms and elements that cross your path?

Does that not speak to your heart of where to dwell
and where to abide in your consciousness?

Does that not spark your soul to lead your life anew?

It is time for all to know that ones are either regenerating or degenerating, in body, mind, spirit. Each one has a lifestyle that regenerates or degenerates. And each must come to know how he or she will live, should one choose to regenerate.

And many will say, in a voice of pity, that it is hard. It is hard to follow this path to return to my True Self, my True Identity as I, the Christ within.

I say clearly to those who would voice these words. It is harder, much harder, and most painful, to continue living out your life in the old way, the way of the human mind, of false beliefs and concepts and opinions. Do not deceive yourselves into believing that it is easier on any level.

The loss of Self is one of the greatest pains.

Do not delude your self. And, know, dear ones, that pity will pull you under. Should you choose to merge with pity, it will swallow you.

Know that you can overcome pity and all your beliefs against your Self…simply by your deepest desire.

Desire to contact your True Self.
Now…

Desire that so much that nothing can hold you back. That desire will open doors, open new worlds. That desire will put you on a road…that you never knew in the ever human mind was even possible or even in existence.

Desire your Self. Desire the Self.
And you shall find…
There is but One Self.
You are that Self. All are that Self.

Begin in the mind's single eye to see the new world.
Begin to imagine the possibilities.
Explore the vast creation before you.
And meditate.
Meditate deeply on Christ,
on truth, on God, on the Buddha Mind,
on the wordless and the nameless.
Enter the never ending NOW…

Open your Consciousness to the truth of I AM.
Open your Consciousness to the truth of your Being.
Open your Consciousness to your Soul's Remembering.
Open your Consciousness to your Soul Mission.

Dear ones…
Open your Eye that you may see.
See the One Vision.
Find your part in that One Vision.
We are here and we are One.

Desire to enter the kingdom.
Desire to experience God.
Desire to realize "I and God are One."
Desire the Oneness.
This desire will lead you to meditation.
And it can only happen now.

January 17, 1999 in Arizona

Dawn Will Come in the Great Embrace

Mary…tell the people this.

Tell them that if a hundred people were to meditate and that if there was a "magic button" to push, to go into meditation, the ones who would easily "make contact" are those who know how to push the button.

It is rather like this. If a man and woman have arrived at the day of their union, their marriage one to the other, they have approached their day, their moment of union as holy.

> They approach with reverence.
> They approach with honoring.
> They approach with the deepest desire for unity.
> They approach the space of marriage as a sanctuary.

> This is their day of days!
> The two come together.
> It is a sacred moment.

> Meditation must be approached as a wedding ceremony.
> It must be approached with reverence.
> You are the lover approaching the beloved.
> You desire union…now…
> You desire oneness…now…
> You are to join with the Christ…
> This moment…now…the holy of holy.
> Is your space prepared before you?
> Is there beauty, silence, reverence in the atmosphere?

You, dear ones, bring all of this to the meditation.
You, dear ones, bring all of this to the wedding.

In your consciousness, live the magic that knows how to push that magic button. It is a state of consciousness.

Your mind must be in a state of consciousness that is ready to be in the presence of the beloved. Your consciousness must be as receptive and open as is the bride to the groom. Your consciousness must long to receive the Christ…the Holy Presence.

In this joining, you will remember I Am.
You will remember I already Am.
And you will remember that I Am Everywhere.
You will remember I Am the only presence here.
You will remember.

Come.
Come now to the wedding.

And many will say to you, I just can't meditate or I'm just not the type to meditate or that is not my way to meditate.

Tell them where they'll find the wedding.
The wedding happens in the Silence.

Invite them into the Silence…beyond the mind…
Invite them to feel the Holy Presence.
Invite them to eat the manna with a circle of gathered Ones.
Invite them to the wedding.
My child, invite them to the wedding.

This message from the silence is an invitation…
an invitation to the wedding.

Only it is, that in this inner wedding shall you find joy in the outer wedding of man and woman. The outer wedding is but a dim remembrance of the Wedding to the One.

> Come…come…come…
> fragrance fills the air…
> The beloved ever awaits…
> Come…

And, Mary, tell the people that the outer physical life that they see and that they live is often a narrow and darkened definition of Life.

> Tell them that their Life
> is an outpouring of their own human definition.
> Tell them it is not Real.
> Nor is it true.
>
> Definitions can be dangerous.
> They can lead one far astray
> down a darkened path to nowhere.
>
> Definitions are given too often
> by those with a need or a motive.

They will ask how they can leave these narrow conceptual definitions and find life that is real.

> Tell them…to come to the wedding…
> Tell them…Light will come during the holy kiss…
> Tell them…dawn will come in the great embrace…
> Tell them…they will awaken out of the human dream…
> in union…
> Tell them…the wedding awaits…

The bells are ringing…
Music can be heard everywhere…
Come…

January 19, 1999 in Arizona

The Fragrance of God

Tell the story of "the fragrance of God"…
that the human concept of aromatherapy might wash away.

In humanity, exists the value of aroma and scent for healing, for therapy. Should, instead, one journey into the sweetest presence, there might come the experience of "the fragrance of God."

Many mornings in my little house at the edge of a forest ridge, I would awaken at predawn and begin to meditate. Into my window God would breathe and I…I would smell God. Outside my window in a thicket of bushes and trees was a family of Shasta Lilies. Each year the family grew and graced me with fragrance from the formless world.

The smell and I…did join.
Joy did fill my soul.

I am not therapy. I do not know of therapy.
To do therapy one must go into separation
and see something wrong.
One need not go there.
One need not.
I am the essence of flower that one smells.
Merge with that fragrance.
Be one with it.
And lift into the sweetest world.
Come…

January 21, 1999 in Arizona

A Mystery No More

Child, you are very resistant to my use of the words, tell the people and tell them. You are certain that ones will be resistant to those words and that it will set up a strong resistance to the message. You fear it will cause them to react the way a child to a parent or authority would act if they did not like how they were being spoken to.

I tell you this, child.
These are the words that I do choose.
I choose them as they are direct.
I use them because it is the way things are.

I use them because…
we are past the time of long stories and veiled truths.

I tell you,
it is time the children come Home.
It is time they realize their Oneness with me.

I tell it in this way for it is time it be heard clearly,
not disguised in any way.

You recently read *The Rubaiyat* by Omar Khayyam, as translated by Paramahansa Yogananda. Until Yogananda had illumined understanding of this famous Persian poem, its meaning has been hidden, cloaked in mystical language that has kept much of it a mystery to the human mind. It is a mystery no more. It can be ignored, but not misunderstood.

I tell you,
it is time the mysteries remove their veils.

We are in that time,
that time of a great collective awakening.

So again, I say, tell them.

January 29, 1999 in Arizona

Life as Simple

Many have asked you how you live alone.
Are you happy…they ask.

Tell them of your Life as Living Ceremony.

Tell them how you eat your breakfast in silence.
Tell them how you love to place your fruits and nuts
before you as a communion.
Tell them how you love to take a pear
and appreciate those who sold it to you,
the store who provided it,
the truckers who transported it,
the pickers who picked it,
the growers who planted the tree…
all the way back to the pear seed…
and then go beyond the seed…
back to the Life that lies dormant in the seed…
and the One Life beyond that.

Tell them that Life as simple has its own joys.
Life as appreciation has its own joys.

Tell them that you love mango juice running
down your mouth and chin.
Tell them you love sticky.
Tell them you love to touch all your food.

Tell them they may sit in front of the morning sky,
light a candle, and smile into the day.

And if they should say, I don't have time,
tell them that once you also did not have time.
Tell them that unhappiness was your lot.
Tell them that you made time.

And tell them you love to pick your apples,
your strawberries, your cherries, your plums.
Tell them that time is what they make of it.

No longer need humanity have others fix their time.
Go within…
and that which is Timeless…
shall gather up your time and place it in your path.

January 29, 1999 in Arizona

The Epiphany Comes...

I awoke at predawn with a dream about *The Epiphany Comes...* I heard those words.

I lay in bed awake for about one and one half hours until dawn in the energy that came in this dream. As I lay there, I heard over and over *The Epiphany Comes...* The energy of it is an ecstatic one...of great love and joy!

I kept waiting for information to come, but none came. When I got up that morning, I looked up *epiphany* in the dictionary. It said: 1) an appearance or manifestation of a god or other supernatural being and 2) in most Christian churches, a yearly festival held January 6th, commemorating the revealing of Jesus as the Christ to the Gentiles in the person of the Magi at Bethlehem; also called The Twelfth Night.

This dream and repeating phrase of *The Epiphany Comes* came the morning after I had been rereading *Starseed Transmissions*, where Ken Carey speaks of the manifestation of angels and extraterrestrials...and The Second Coming. I opened the doors of my consciousness to this event. It is The Epiphany. We are in it. It is happening now...and with that realization came these words...from the wordless realm...

* The use of the word Christ in the following transmission is not referencing a person. It is speaking of a state of Divine Consciousness... a state of holy Presence, available to all. The word, Christ, transcends religions. Christ, Krishna, and Buddha all refer to the Light and bliss of the God Mind. They are referring to a state of illumination and enlightenment. It is fully impersonal.

The Epiphany is happening.
It is a far reaching event.
It not only circles the Earth, but enters all consciousness.
It will either raise a person to great heights…or they will fall.
They will fall into the mire of their own miscreation.

The Epiphany is a great event.
It has been awaited by everyone…consciously or unconsciously.
Many have misinterpreted and mistranslated
the energies of this great event.
Many see Armageddon because they see amiss.
They see amiss because of their human beliefs and concepts.
Those who have glimpsed this sacred time
of revelation through meditation,
through entering the silence,
have glimpsed The Epiphany.
And it is Now.

The occurrence of the manifestations will increase as time goes by.
The amount of Light on Earth will increase as a result.
How life is viewed will change radically.
Change will be welcomed finally.

We are the Living Book of Changes.
We are the Living Revelations.
We are the flowing of the River of Life.

The Epiphany is the return of the Christ…
the holy presence…
It is The Second Coming.
It is the Revelation of that truth in the hearts of all.
Those in denial or resistance will have a most difficult time.
Compassion must encircle them as they "run their resistance."
That resistance will begin to burn and sear.

There is no running away from The Epiphany.
This is the time.
Now…is the time…

Child, you will continue to receive information
on The Epiphany.
Ever increasing numbers are now in place.
Their desire for Oneness in the Christ
has unfolded their present position.

The greatest danger during the next years
is "looking to appearances."
The awakening ones must train themselves
to see everyone beyond the human identity.
Humanity must see all others in their true identity,
regardless of their human errors.

The consciousness of those who can see others and everything
in the Light of the Christ
will have an uplifting effect on all those they meet.
This is changing the greeting of Namaste
into an actual occurrence of consciousness.
Those who are open and receptive
will be lifted out of the human problems and miscreations.
They, in turn, must learn how to shift their consciousness,
that they do not recreate the problem.

Disasters are creations of the human mind.

The Epiphany marks the departure from the human sense of things.
It marks the entrance of a new age.
This age will be known as one of Light.
An Age of Light.

This awareness of Light will transcend any human dreams.
It cannot be imagined, for it is outside the human mind.
This awareness of Light will bring and is revealing…
unprecedented joy,
unprecedented unions,
unprecedented creations.

The Epiphany draws all unto the Light.
This Light will reveal life on and with this planet,
beyond what human languaging can even say.

The Epiphany will reveal the Light of the Christ as an experience,
not something to read or study or talk about.
All the reading and studying has been a preparation.
It has readied the human consciousness
to expand to this vast Consciousness.
It has made the human mind a fertile garden
to plant the seed of desire.

Ever larger numbers desire Oneness in the Light.
Oneness with the Christ.
That experience of Oneness,
whether grand or a tiny glimpse
reveals Oneness with Creator and creation.

Human emotions and beliefs are translated into rapture.
The human emotions and beliefs are energies that are stuck.
The Oneness experience dissolves the "stuck energy"
and retranslates and reveals the truth.

All of history, as we currently know it, will be flushed.
It is not based on Truth.
Humanity will learn that civilization after civilization
has fallen…because it was built on lies.

One cannot build a culture, a cult or gathering of light,
based on a false premise.

Any civilization that begins with a false premise begins with a lie.
And it will fall.

Look about you now, each in your own nation.
You will see what is not working.
You will see what is starting to fall.

Dictators to heads of state fall…
simply because they lead a nation with lies.

People have been told…
"know the Truth and the Truth will set you free."
One cannot want control and freedom at the same time.

The Light of Truth…borning in humanity now…
will bring structures built by lies to dissolution.
The sheer numbers of those of light will expose the lies.
The lies will fall.
Lies have no reality.
Humanity has unknowingly supported lies.
That time is passing.
It is passing fast.

The Epiphany gains momentum.
The experience of Oneness is the passage
into conscious awareness of The Epiphany.

Discern, in all aspects of your living,
if you are in the grace of Oneness.
If not, be willing to change your thoughts, your activities, your ways.

Each individual change accelerates the global change.
Each individual alignment with the truth
is more light on the planet.

Each individual in the Christ light of oneness
is in contact with the One Power, that is God.
Humanity living in the dark
has no conscious contact with the One Power.
They can only muster up false power
through control, force, and manipulation
of peoples and their minds and events of their lives.

Give no power to these atrocities.
Believe not in that which is a lie.
And the lies will fall.
Fear has no basis in truth.

Behold…The Epiphany comes…

February 3, 1999 in Mount Shasta, California

The Giver of Grace

Lo…I am here. I come this evening in first person.
I have given forth the great Law of Forgiveness
as a most important law throughout the ages.
I have said forgive debts, trespasses;
I have said forgive the enemy.
Forgive…I have said…forgive.
Let me tell you why I have taught you to forgive.

To forgive is to come into Grace.
To forgive is to dissolve the bonds of karma.
To forgive is to fulfill the Law of Balance.
Ponder these words well.
In them is a great key to the mastery…
known as grace…

Should you break the karmic return through forgiveness,
you would return unto the Father's House.
It is I awaiting…as the giver of grace.

You will not waste your time on earth plane,
should you ponder deeply this great magic
unveiled through forgiveness.

You will waste not your time,
should you observe well the effects in your life, through forgiveness.

Ponder well its power of dissolution of miscreated relationships.

Ponder well…I say…

February 3, 1999 in Mount Shasta, California

Experience with the Plant Kingdom

I was driving to Arizona and a beautiful moment happened on the I-5 interstate highway. I drove past what seemed to be about a mile of trees in full bloom, on both sides of the highway. I could feel the emanations from the blossoms. Presence. It was like driving through the finest, most gossamer energy streams of love. My perception of life force through creation became heightened as I drove through those trees. Magic in the air.

Later, I drove into Sedona, Arizona and stopped on town business. Outside the building was a tree in full pink bloom. I felt the heightened perception again…as I could feel and sense the light glow from the blossoms. In addition, the delicate scent was pouring forth, adding to the moment of expansion and opening. I felt I had just entered a special and magical garden.

We are here. Together. In the garden.

February 5, 1999 in Arizona

Masquerading Defenses

Dear Child, you are to understand defenses.
When humanity, as you know it, went into separation,
it went into the knowledge of good and bad, duality.
When humanity began to judge things as good and bad,
it was an obvious next step to defend oneself
from that which it deemed bad or even evil.
So the battle of evil began
and all manner of defenses and armor ensued,
even to huge walls and fortresses being built around areas.
Berlin had a wall of defense.
The cavalry had forts of defense.
The defense humanity created individually
was much more subtle and vague
and difficult to perceive.
So masterful has humanity become
at masquerading its defenses.

The important note here is that
when one comes into the presence of God,
one comes out of the sense of separation,
back to Source.
The need for defense drops away.
The past need for defense falls away.
The past falls away.
The need to analyze falls away.

In the presence, all is forgiven.
Grace begins to do her dance.

February 10, 1999 in Arizona

The Stream of Oneness

Dear Child, the experience you had with the birds is a new level of Oneness. It will continue. The Oneness experiences you have had in meditation and in the Archetypal realms for many years will now reach new levels when your eyes are opened, when you are actually out in the world.

A shift point has occurred. The Stream of Oneness into your physical universe is ready to expand.

When you were driving to Sedona and saw the huge grouping of 200–300 birds fly from one side of the road to the other, you tapped in to their collective energy and experience. You felt not only their Oneness, but their collective expression of Oneness. You felt the ecstasy of that energy. You felt the waves and currents from their movements enter your own being. In that merge, you all shared the same experience.

These are the delights that await humanity as it merges with Creator and Creation. It is why you are inspired to share "the merge experience" in art, in poetry, in sessions, retreats, and multimedia events.

Upon these times we are in, it is important that humanity know how to stay in Oneness with Source, with Creator, that it can merge then with the glories of creation. Not just her physical Beauty, but the energy, the essence and nectar of Her expressions.

This will in turn fine tune people, so that they do not merge with the human emotions borne of a sense of separation from Source and then need to act those out.

*Following is a brief description of the experience with the birds.
February 8, 1999.*

Late morning, I am driving to Sedona. I see them ahead. I see 200–300 birds.

Large swarms of small dark birds…appear before me…flying quickly from one side of the road to the other. They fly in group undulations…wave patterns that can be easily felt.

> I merge with the energy of their waves…
> I can feel it…I am it…
> Joy…life…courses through my veins…
> courses through my being…
> I am lifting…

I looked for a place to pull off the road. I could not find one; a car was just behind me. I thought I'd find one just after I passed the birds, so I could stop and watch and feel. The moment I passed by, they flew away.

> I knew that was for my eyes…to behold…
> It was for my being…to feel…
> I felt light, buoyant, happy…

(*Note: Mary Saint-Marie has been doing Soul Merging Retreats with others since the 80's. She assists others to merge into Oneness with Creator and Creation/Nature. And Knowing…it comes. The work is Galactic Shamanism: Journey through the Kingdoms and Journey through the Elements.*)

Vision…silent on your tongue…

Tell of the vision you saw many years ago…
Tell of the vision you carry silent on your tongue…

Tell finally that a day will come
when collisions will no longer happen
upon the roads across the lands…

Tell of that day when fear does leave the hearts…
of all in whom it dwells…

Tell of the day when only love is on the road of Life…
And collisions happen not…

Tell the story that love knows…

Where love is…collision does not come…
…collision does not exist…
Collision is the effect of fear
dwelling in the hearts.
And fear breeds emotions of the fiercest kind…
And emotions have ruled many a road…
on Earth's grand lands…
And soon…does come the day when that is past…
Collisions end…when love does come…
And love does rule the road…

With love…comes awareness…
…comes understanding…
…comes caring…
Caring will rule the road…

The Road is a metaphor here for Life as well.
Caring will fill our lives.

So watch ourselves behind the wheel...
Who is driving?
The emotions of fear...
or the feelings of love?

Each time we turn that key...
know who will drive the car that day...

Remember...Love comes...

February 12, 1999 in Arizona

Visitors…in time…

I cast shadows in my coming…
but only for a while…
The day shall come…
when light shall stream
in everything that is…

Shadows…they shall fall away…
They were visitors in time…
with a role on this grand stage…
But soon they'll go…

And on the stage…
new actors come…
A brilliance never known…

A play does come…
that could not dwell…
cased in shadows from the past…

A play does come…
that sits upon all hearts and shouts…
Rejoice…the lord is come…

February 12, 1999 in Arizona

Faraway Shores

I travel now to faraway shores…
looking for unopened hearts…

For them I prepare…
a scene of delight…
a scene that touches deep…

Lonely and alone…despair has reached its peak…
when they do come…
in the forest deep…
upon a new born fawn…
She suckles on her mother's breast…
Peace does fill the air…

Despair does die…
and peace does dwell instead…
Love begins to fill the heart…

I begin to weep…

I weep in wonder…
as my children…
do drink upon my life…

February 12, 1999 in Arizona

Flowers Speaking from the Silence

Child…there will come a new day.
In that new day the joy and beauty of flowers
will be experienced in new ways.

No longer will flowers be used for therapy.
Their essences will not be squeezed for gaining wellness.
I speak of a time when Life will be experienced,
not from the point of view of sickness and wellness
and all the therapy approaches,
but from wholeness…and rapture even…

When that time does come,
there will be no desire to take the life of the flowers for anything.
Their lives will be enjoyed for just that…their lives.

During this time of healing and regeneration,
flowers are being used for all sorts of assistance.
From cosmetic beauty, to dyes,
for flower essences and perfumes, for bouquets.

All these uses take the life of the flower.
If you will, take a moment and imagine this new day.
Imagine this day of n'er taking the life of a flower.
What are the changes your soul does see?

The lives of flowers will no longer be sacrificed
for our health, our balance, our beauty, or scent.

Why is it we would smear a petal upon our lip?
What is it we have lost?

O children of the earth…I ask you to entertain these thoughts.
Follow this essence from the flowers back into the invisible
and find that for which you seek in colored lips and cheeks.

This idea is a stretch.
But I promise it will take you to the other side
of "healing consciousness."
It will begin one's shift into the vastness
of Wholeness consciousness.

Begin to see and be aware of a new relationship with the flowers.
Ask to hear them sing.
Ask to smell their sweetest scent
from the consciousness of wholeness.
Ask to experience their essence as they glow
from trees, bushes, stems…

They have great mystery to reveal.
They have unprecedented messages from the invisible world.
They share in sound, color, smell…great essence.

Gardens everywhere will come forth.
Big gardens. Little gardens.
City gardens. Country gardens.
People will see these as ashrams, centers, and sacred sites.

The flowers speak loudly from the Silence
to all those who begin to experience Oneness.

This message is an invitation to entertain some new thoughts.
Out of the Silence of Oneness…these thoughts will flow to you.
In your very yard, you may create now…this new day…

March 11, 1999 while driving to Flagstaff, Arizona

I Am the Wedding Day

Child, I am your Beloved…the one you call so much…
I am your Lover…the one you do await…
I am the Lover and Beloved…
I am the Wedding Day…
I am the union…of the day and of the night…
I am the caller and the one who's called…
I am the viewer and the viewed…
For me there is no Heaven and Earth…
For me there is just here…
Here I am…nowhere else exists
except in a mind that has no truth…

Let it be known that you are mine alone…
You are One that I did choose…
Each known moment of your life
shall enter from the Mystery…
Your trust is mine and we do celebrate…
Your smile spreads across your face
and light does glint across your eyes…

Wedded…we do walk…and play
in joy upon the lands…
Wedded…we do see eternal shores
and lightly step upon Earth's sands…
Wedded…we are one throughout the world
with all who come our way…
Wedded…we shall explore the universe
bringing truth to all who will…

April 2, 1999 in Arizona

Come Child...

How do the rich get richer and the poor get poorer? What kind of imbalance lies at the root of our current society? Is it that the rich are preying upon the poor? What is the cause of it? Is it that the rich work hard and the poor don't? Actually, often the opposite is so. From where does such inequality come? Why has it been allowed?

Child, at the root of both of these imbalances is fear!
Both fear that they will not have enough.
This fear in both extremes is born of separation from Me.
Oneness with me means abundance...
having...with no fear.
Coming back home is the answer.
Come child.

April 5, 1999 in Arizona

Friends...you are creation...

Tell the people this. Come to me, children. It matters not what happens when you sit in the Silence. Sitting in the Silence is like plugging your plug into the socket. You are now connected. You now have set your intent. You have now surrendered to Source. You have now said yes to Self, the One Self. Now, you can begin to hear new ideas, meet new people, create from new levels. Never believe that nothing happened in meditation. Situations can now find their way into your life easily, without a struggle, as you are plugged into the Infinite circuitry of Creation.

Ponder this idea. Think about it. Contemplate it. You will see that it makes perfect sense. For if you make yourself "consciously" a part of the Whole that Creation is, then you become increasingly aware of your part of the outplay of that Creation.

> Friends, you are Creation.
> You are more than just creative.
> You are the baker and the bread.

In meditation, you shall find your Oneness with Creator. You shall soar to new levels of relatings with humans, minerals, plants, animals, and the elements. You shall have new relatings with the weather and the climate. You shall cease opposing weather and always trying to get it to fit neatly into your personal plans. When you begin to find your consciousness flowing with "what is," you shall find yourself in "perfect weather patterns." You shall find yourself in the garden. And you shall fall on your knees in joy and lightheartedness...knowing this has always been here...awaiting your awareness.

> I greet you…in all ways.
> I greet you everywhere you turn.
> Recognize me thus.

And, Mary, tell the people this. Tell them I shall whisper in their ears as the sun does cross upon the sky. And tell them that as the day does pass before their eyes, that I shall be there, living through them, as them, as they allow. Separation is in the mind. It is no other place. It is a thought in the great confusion of the human mind.

> Dwell no longer in this sad place.
> Dwell no longer in this angry place.
> Dwell no longer in this fearful place.
> Come, children, dwell ever in my house.

Here you shall find the riches of love, of peace and overflowing awareness.

April 29, 1999 in Mount Shasta, California

Inheritance

Stress is a disease in our culture
borne of separation from Spirit.

That disease is fear.

Fear lives and breeds where there is no trust in the Infinite. There is no trust in the Infinite where there is a sense of separation.

We have separated God/Love from almost everything.
We have separated church and state.
We have even separated God from business and from the schools.

Is it no wonder there is violence? Even our media, our movies, our novels are filled with the fascination of pathology.

Why should we be surprised when our children act out our creations of culture? Seeing the culture is how they learn.

We have taught them amiss. We have fed them guns, bombs, wars, murder, speed, suicides, in both fact and in fiction.

And we expect Grace.

These children are in fear.
The fear borne of separation from Creator, from the Infinite.
We have made them heirs of fear.
A poor and paltry inheritance.

In truth, they have another inheritance.
It lies waiting in their hearts.
And there the sense of separation ends.

June 6, 1999 in Mount Shasta, California

Harmony: Archetypal Goddess of the Ecosystem

We are living in a time of much information. Many people have studied the environment in this beautiful world about us and learned much about the ecosystem. Thanks to these people, we all finally know much about the science of the interconnectedness of minerals, plants, animals, and the air, earth, fire, and water.

That connectedness can also be known through the feelings and intuition. And that connectedness of the ecosystem is not "out there." We, too, are that ecosystem. The relatedness with which we "feel" depends on our ability to attune to our Oneness with Creation. Our Oneness with Creation is the ecosystem. And that Oneness is the projection of Creator into the earthplane, that we call Home.

Let us relook at our role in this exquisite ecosystem. That ecosystem is the Universal Order.

Though we have scientific, environmental, religious, academic, and artistic ways of speaking does not mean we are talking about different things.

Regardless of the names and intellectual meanings with which we tag the Higher Order, we are all still speaking about the Wordless and the Nameless. With that realization, we will all be on the same wavelength. We will all know we speak of the same thing, though we give it different names.

Let us not allow the different names to keep us as separate in our minds. That is the only place that separation does exist.

Our relatedness is Relatedness. We are all related. We are related to all the kingdoms and elements and forces through Nature. This is why the native peoples refer to "all my relations." They know of their Oneness with Nature. Even the children do know…

With this in mind, let us reconsider the nature of all our relationships. Let us call for our own direct knowing of the Truth of our Relationships.

With Relatedness as a focus in the education of humanity, our world would see a most magnificent shift and change. Harmony would again unveil Herself. SHE has never been far away. HER distance can only be measured in the thoughts or beliefs that have seemed to keep us in separation.

Why is this so? For everything on the Earth can be described in terms of Principle. That Principle is the operation of Oneness, regardless of our beliefs or concepts. When we approach Life as a Principle, we can begin to enjoy our differences of description, view, explanation, etc. And Harmony…SHE shall do her Dance…

June 13, 1999 while driving from Mount Shasta to Seattle

This Wedding...

This wedding embraces all traditions and cultures
that have ever been, that are, and will ever be...

This wedding embraces true love
between man and woman everywhere...

This wedding embraces true love
between the masculine and feminine,
the yin and yang in all of Nature,
in all the mated opposites,
in all the kingdoms,
in the elements,
in the conditions of weather...

We live...in an electrically sexed universe of the opposites, divine complements ever moving toward one another, in a powerful Dance of the One reuniting with Itself...

Friends...
we are that union...
we all are that union...

Together...
let us celebrate that union of the sacred two,
given from Creator,
and come together as the One...

Yet paradoxically,
they are still the two...

In this, the mystery stands unveiled...

that we may feel the Presence of this wedding…
this holy union of yin and yang…
of this single man and woman
and in the grander scheme of things…

Together…let us celebrate…

August 29, 1999 in Mount Shasta, California

Abide in Me

I am the invisible presence that is everywhere.
I Am all things.
I fill and surround all things.
I am everywhere, yet nowhere.
I am the living paradox.

Abide in me.

I am the action and the non-action.
There is nowhere that I am not found.

I am the alpha and the omega
and all that is in between...

Abide in me.

In truth, you abide in me whether you know it or not.
In these times, abide in me consciously.

You can have a neon sign
and if you do not switch it on, it cannot do its job.
You are like that.

Abide in me.

October 11, 1999 in Mount Shasta, California

This River

Humanly, we say, change is hard. It is true; humanly, change is hard. For humanly, we are in fear. Out of fear, we do everything to control our lives. We control and manipulate our lives to make them safe, secure, and stable. Safe, secure, stable. Those keep us out of fear. So we become left brained, linear, logical, and reasonable. And we begin to die. To stagnate. To live in pathology.

For change is Life. And Life is energy, flow; it is the power of God, Itself, flowing through creation. Creator as creation. That is Life. Flowing, changing, life giving, dynamic, powerful. And to the human mind, that is scary. It is out of control.

So how is it that we jump into Life? How is it that we humans leave scary and fear behind? For fear paralyzes and constipates our lives. It stops the flow of this great energy through us. Fear is the human mind in separation.

There is only, simply, Source or separation. Source is Love. Separation is fear. Source is Life. A sense of separation is pain and suffering borne of no movement, no flow of Life Itself.

How is it that we move from a fear based and fear oriented life to a love based life, a joy based life?

We can begin by going into Nature. Watch the flow of Life in the daily, moment by moment, changing of the seasons. Watch the flow of Life in the minerals, the plants, the animals. Watch the flow of Life through the elements of earth, air, fire, and water. Life is always moving, always changing.

Creation changes as energy, Spirit, Presence flows through it, as it.

But Creator, It is changeless. It is eternal Creator. How do we tap this eternal Creator that is the Source of all things, that we may leave fear behind?

We can turn our mind from fear, which is sense of separation from the Source, and turn our awareness to the Truth, to what Is. We can turn the mind to dwell in the eternal Now. Fear rests in the past or future.

We can let go of all our concepts, all our beliefs, and go deep within ourselves, into the Silence. This Silence, this zero point, is the power of the universe. It is where all our dreams do dwell. It is the place of Vision. It is the source, the headwaters of the River we know as Life.

Contact that Source.
Feel its Presence.
Feel those currents flow through you.

Jump into that River of Life,
knowing it will give you all you ever wanted.

It will fulfill your desires.
It will answer your questions.
It will give you solutions to problems.
It will transform obstacles into opportunities
and doors of new understanding.
It will literally translate fear into love.

For fear is a lie. Fear is never based on truth. Fear is a false concept, a false belief that we somehow bought. And if we bought it, it is ours. We may not even buy it consciously. We buy it because it is a thought floating, insidiously, through the same air waves that give us radios, telephones, televisions, computers, satellites, psychic abilities. Fear is the lower astral plane that lingers as lies in our airwaves, keeping us ever in the human spell. And because we dwell in a thought wave universe, a light wave universe, thoughts are things.

We must become guardians at the door of our minds, of our consciousness. We must choose the thoughts consciously that dwell in our minds, our temples.

Fear thoughts are miscreations. They are lies. They are not the truth. The only thing that sustains and maintains them is our scary belief in them. We, ourselves, turn them unknowingly into dragons, demons, devils that stop the flow of the River of Life, that is Love, through us.

The perpetuators of fear would have it thus. Most civilizations of history have been fear based. Innocent love-filled babies are born into these historical lies.

One by one, we can turn these lies, these fears, around. When a fear, any fear, arises, we can turn to the Source of all creation. We can go into the Silence and feel the Presence of Spirit. And we can open to its flow through our minds, bodies, hearts. We can, in trust, turn our awareness there to feel this awesome Presence that is Life. Your Life. My Life. All Life. There is only one Life. Oneness.

Feel this Oneness flow through your veins.
Feel the joy.
Feel the ecstasy.

Intuition will come. Follow it.
Guidance will come. Follow it.
Life will reveal itself. Follow it.
Allow this River to flow through your very veins.

We all have free will. And there may be certain ones who choose for the moment to stay in the prison of fear. Let them go. Their time will come and they too will let go of the branches they grasp that keep them on the bank, watching the River of they know not what.

This River is the life giver, the gift bringer. It brings the unprecedented. It brings the seeming miracles. It lives only in the now, the eternal present moment. It is spontaneous and it knows no limits, no boundaries. It is the ever sought Eden, the paradise.

It is a state of consciousness. And our entry into this state of consciousness, this presence, is awareness. It, this River, is already here. We must find our way through awareness. We must be open…receptive to it…through prayer, meditation, becoming still, and entering that Silence. It speaks.

Then, we begin a journey, a great odyssey of realization. That journey is the journey to our Self.

We begin to realize our Self. And we begin to realize there is only one Self. Creator as creation. That is who we are. The awakening begins. We begin to move out of slumber. We begin to Remember. And we are thrilled. Our bodies thrill to this Presence. Our minds thrill to this Presence. Even our emotions are thrilled.

And we begin to intuit what to do, where to be. The answers seem to come before we have a question.

And one day we realize the current in this River is getting stronger. We realize we are getting stronger. The strength, the Light, that is this Presence, is us. We begin to experience a great paradox. That Life is us. God, Spirit, is us, appearing as light bringers.

How could that be?
Look out at history.
Look back through the ages, my child,
at the fear based civilizations.

Fear translates into wars, savagery, barbaric practices, patriarchy, control over others, imbalance, pathologies. Fear breeds no child but suffering. Fear is a tragic ruler.

From fear to love.
That is the journey.
Begin the journey now.

It is a journey of consciousness. It is a sacred journey. And you will receive the highest degree of education available in the cosmos.

Do not be in regret or shame of the fears you have or have had. They are/have been your teachers.

And be grateful, my child, that you have experienced such great depths of this fear. This fear that is not you, nor is it true.

This fear…it has given you gifts. Great gifts that you could receive in no other way. You know first hand the ravages of fear upon a life. You know the pathologies of the mind that begin to appear. You know the subtle and insidious nature of fear's call. You have gained compassion. You understand others still frozen in the fear, borne of a sense of separation from Spirit.

Our history records the lives of many souls who knew no better. They followed fear's call and entered the astral realms of hell, which is no more than a mind distorted with miscreation.

Let not your mind linger on fear's trail. Give your mind to the

Light. Be filled with Light. That Light that is the marriage of love and wisdom. It is the holy wedding that happens in your very consciousness.

Begin to pray, my child. Pray unceasingly, that your path of Light be revealed. There are many paths. You are the magic genie that can unlock your Aladdin's lamp. And the awareness of the consciousness of the Presence is the key and the door.

October 24, 1999, written at dawn

I am the grasses and the grapes…

Stress is fear. And our culture is full of stress. We manage stress. We cope with stress. We die of stress. Stress destroys the immune system. The body has no way to defend itself. Stress becomes the name of the game of life. Fun leaves. Joy flees.

Life becomes a daily act of stress and coping. We eat to cope. We drink to cope. We have sex to cope. We work out to cope. We run. We exercise.

All these measures are temporary. They affect the effects of stress. They do not get at the cause.

The cause is separation. The cause is separation from Spirit. Sense of separation from Self. Your Self. Your true Self.

The act of separation takes place in the mind and affects the emotions and the body. The act of separation is an act of slow death. It is slow and it is full of pain.

Our culture has been living out the act of separation. And it is a lie.

A culture of stress…is a culture built on lies.

That act of separation is a departure from the Presence. Fear is found in the past and the future where our culture dwells.

In the Presence of the present moment is found Joy. Our culture is built on the past and the future and we have left the

Joy. In its place is stress, no immune system and slow death.

How do we return to this Presence of the present moment? We return one at a time. Person by person. And we return by going into the Stillness. There we will find the timeless Presence that never changes. There we will find wholeness. Not healing, but wholeness. In Presence, the need for healing never happened. In Presence, Joy is. Joy does not become. Joy just is.

What is this Joy of which ones speak? What is this Joy that just IS, when one no longer dwells in the stress, the fear borne of separation?

Name that Joy any name you want. God, Source, Illumination, Christ, Buddha mind, Divine Mind, and on. It is the nameless and the wordless. Humans giving it a name does not change the It! For It is the changeless. And because it is the timeless, it will not be found in time.

So here we all are sitting here in time. How will we find this Joy? We are caught, trapped and imprisoned in time, it seems.

We will use our consciousness to make a journey. We will make a journey from time into the timeless, that is, from sense of separation to Source, from stress to Joy. Or we may name that Joy…love, peace, bliss, samadhi, rapture, and on…

The game of naming can go on and on. When we are through naming, we can enter into the nameless experience. The intellect cannot take hold, nor can it travel there.

The intellect is a tool, an instrument, a sweetest vessel of Spirit. When intellect is activated and animated with the light of truth, the motivation and the inspiration for action…it shifts. It shifts from fear based to love based. The orientation shifts from stress to expression of one's Self.

For in this timeless stillness lies waiting your very own awareness of Self. That Self is a spark of the Divine. The Oneness that knows no other. The Oneness that knows Joy.

And in this timeless stillness, the mind remembers. It begins to remember. It remembers who it is and why it came. It remembers laughter. It smiles. It does not fight with itself. And it sees only Itself. It is everywhere.

It says, I alone Am. I am everywhere present. I am everywhere. I am the trees. I am the grasses and the grapes. I am the sand along the beach. I am the face upon the fish and the eyes in the lion that roams. I am the snake that slithers across the ground. And I am the ground it slithers on. I am the fire of the suns, the moisture upon your brow. I am everywhere seen. Yet I am unseen. I am the unformed Presence, waiting to play in form.

> *Stress is a lie. Leave the lie.*
> *Enter this moment of now.*
> *Enter it now.*
> *Enter it alone.*
> *There…will be found…alone exists not.*
> *Alone…it never was…*
> *Alone is all one…*
> *We are all one…*
> *And we have been living a lie.*
> *The lie causes stress.*
> *And we can leave the lie.*

The lie is left by going within and finding the Presence. Desire deeply to enter this Presence. The word desire is being used here, instead of prayer, in case we have an atheist among us. It is amazing how we use words to keep us in separation. Words have become a major tool to create separation, thus stress and fear. So desire the Presence. And realize that only in Presence will you experience Joy. That Joy is God.

And the Presence stretches into eternity. The omnipresent. It is everywhere Present. Even in our imagined future, though we have limited it in time.

Let us each be a part of the emerging new culture. The cult of UR. The gathering of light. Culture is the ancient word of the gathering of light.

Our current civilizations have certainly not been cultures. They have been warring and barbaric gangs. They have been savage, including our own current present world. Perhaps more than most. For we can do bigger and more hideous devastation.

How can we leave stress and be a part of the emerging culture of light? One person at a time. We enter one by one. We leave separation and we return to the timeless One. We do this ultimate pilgrimage, not on a mountaintop, but in our consciousness. We may be guided to a mountaintop, but the journey inward, the odyssey Home is in the inner Consciousness. It is in the inner awareness of the nameless, the silence, the stillness.

Even a glimpse, a tiny glimpse of this stillness, can deeply change our lives. We can feel this ever present Presence. And It begins to change our life. Change comes.

We must allow. Allow It to return peace and love and joy to our lives. At our center, we are those very qualities. They are who we are. They are who we Already are.

And we are holy. And we are light. And Joy is all around.

Together…let us be in that Joy…

For those who would still ask…how do I find this Presence… I would say yet again…go within. Some people in western world have a resistance to the word meditate. Don't let words be your excuse to gift yourself with this exquisite experience of Self, your true Self. Don't keep the experience from yourself because of a semantic battle or because you say you are too active.

Let that active part, that activity of life, be catalyzed and animated by Life. True Life flows as a river from the stillness within. Make contact with the stillness. Let it flow through your veins and mind.

> *Your life will be Life.*
> *And your life will know Joy.*
> *And vision will be borne anew.*

That vision is the new emerging culture. It is a culture of light. And it is borne anew. In truth, it has always been there. Waiting, just waiting, to be seen. And with one person at a time, it is being seen.

When it is seen, it can be lived.

Together…let us live this Life and let this Life live us.

> *Cry out in the night if you need.*
> *"Life…live me. Live through me and as me."*
> *And open. Open to the flow of that Life.*
> *Feel it in your body as new action.*
> *Feel it in your mind as new thoughts.*
> *Feel it in your emotions as ecstatic joy!*

Let nothing smother that feeling. Let no job, let no relationship, let no business smother that feeling.

> Together…let us build a culture of Joy.
> A culture that knows no stress, no fear, no lies.
> Let us allow that culture to emerge.
> It is the rising phoenix we have all awaited.

Until now life has been as a dress rehearsal with the wrong script. We must one by one journey into our depths to find our script. There it lies, awaiting our awareness. It is a script of spontaneity. It knows no past, no dead patterns of fear based constructs and configurations and posturings of old. It is of the Presence.

> And it awaits…our remembering.

> Together…let us remember.

And to all this some will say, "I have no trust." Well, trust will not come by itself. It is borne of experience. It is borne of feeling this Presence, the very substance of creation. Then is acquired the gift of direct experience, of direct knowing. That can never be taken away. Trust is borne through contact with the Presence that dwells in the stillness. From there one begins to recognize the feeling. One remembers. One realizes…It is everywhere Present.

> And it will say…*I Am the only Presence Here…*

> And in this holy moment,
> the muscles relax, the tension leaves, and there is a great sigh.
> Exhaustion disappears; stress dissolves.
> For fear has no place to dwell.
> Fear becomes a homeless one.

And it exists not.
It is only a memory in the mind…
to be forgotten as a troubled dream…

And It will say…*I Am the only Presence here…*

December 23, 1999 in Mount Shasta, California

Manes flying...

Friends, we buy cards, posters, art, and books of horses. The tails are flying. Head is lifted. Power flies through space. Horse flying...as the wind...across open spaces. Beauty and power in union in this grand form.

And then we drive down the highways and down the streets and roads of our town and nation. We see horses standing. For hours they do stand. For days and weeks and years. There is no space. There is no space to run as the wind. Small fenced in places everywhere for these grand forms.

Those images on the cards...manes flying through the sky. In many places and with many horses, that is a dream long dead. A fantasy. I dare say...it is criminal to put a horse in a stall or a small space.

Hearts break. But a new day dawns. History only shall know the sight of horses in small spaces standing so still with neck down. Often even alone. With Spirit broken. With Spirit gone.

O this day, let us see the horses again running free in endless miles of open space. Spirit flying in this grand form.

December 24, 1999 while driving to Sacramento, California

O Humanity

O Humanity…sweet humanity…
I call to you…
I call to you through the trees.
I call to you in the wind…
I call to you from everywhere…
Do you hear?
Do you hear, sweet ones?
I Am HERE…
I am in your hearts…
And I am everywhere about…
See me thus…

See me…
Hear me…
and feel me…
I am calling you…

It is time for us to rendezvous…
Let us play in all the ways…
Play with each other…
Even play in your work…

We shall know one another…
and we shall be glad…
O humanity…we shall be glad…

Everywhere see my face…
And…be glad…

My face illumines endless faces…
And…be glad…

I come with Purpose…
And gladness fills the air…
Smiles do fill the Light of Day…
and laughter fills the Night…
See me thus…

Feel me in your kin
and in those far away…
Feel me in your cities
and in the ages past…

I hide nowhere…
I am here…everywhere…

A new day does dawn in this age…
Gladness fills the very air…

Breathe…in recognition…
And sleep shall fall from in your eyes…

O Humanity…hear my sweet whispers…
and join me in this day…

January 5, 2000 in Mount Shasta, California

Vessel of the Infinite

Never mind, for a moment, child abuse, animal abuse, woman and wife abuse, indigenous abuse, Nature abuse. Let us look at body abuse. Look at what we are doing to ourselves. We have created a need for hospitals, drugs, doctors, foundations for every kind of disease. Why are we a disease riddled civilization? Why does it get worse and ever worse? Are we dumb or are we ignorant?

Why have we chosen this level of body abuse? Done by ourselves. Why haven't we opened our eyes…and our minds…to see that what we are doing is not working?

Why haven't we asked the question…for what is this body designed? What food shall I put in this sacred vessel? What is my perfect diet or food? Not because we read about the latest faddish diet of extremes, but because we know what is pure and natural. For what is this body designed?

One only needs to look at the statistics to see that western civilization's degree of body abuse is staggering. And then we take our abusive diet into other cultures and spread our toxic ways.

This abuse can change very fast as, one person at a time, we ask…for what food is my body designed? Each of us carries that knowledge. We may have to dig deep inside to find our knowledge. Our knowing from the Silence.

The result of that search is rapturous existence inside this vessel of the Infinite, which we call a body. This body is a form…it is energy. Let us not pervert, distort, or limit this energy by the miscreations that are a billion dollar business in our civilization. Let us leave a society of lies and be a part of the growing culture of Light.

Let it be...

May 5, 2000 in Mount Shasta, California

This Timeless Flow

In that humanity has frozen time…stopped time…
time has seemed to slow down…stagnate…
All of this has been done in the name of fear.
In the name of separation.

Separation from the Timeless One.

As more and more of humanity Return to the One, time will seem to go faster. Even the expression "time is flying" will be heard around the globe.

What in truth is happening is that Life is being noticed. The flow of Life (God) is being experienced and felt.

As people attune to the Timeless, they will notice the "seeming" change of time. It is in reality the noticing of Life, of Reality, flowing through the outer seeming. The finite sense of the world will begin to fall away…as the Infinite presents its joyful Presence.

This holy oneness…
this holy presence is fully present in the now…
outside of all time…

This timeless flow carries only joy and magic.
The common expression "get in the flow" is profound and timely.

It is time. Now is the Time.
Together…come into the Oneness…

May 2000 at 6:30 a.m. in Mount Shasta, California

Mystic Marriage

We call the mystical…extraordinary.
That which is natural, ordinary, normal…
Is Life…

We are the ones living in an altered state…
that which has been controlled…tampered with…manipulated…
altered until it is almost unrecognizable…
and we try to call it etiquette and polite and reasonable…
and social order…

The paradox is fully missed.
The magic…it is lost…
Innocence and wonder…are fully lost…

The paradox…
Where the ordinary meets extraordinary…
magic happens…
Where normal and paranormal do marry…
magic happens…
Where seen and unseen do marry and meet…
there magic does happen…

Let us leave this altered state…
Let us enter the ordinary and in it find extraordinary…
Let us enter the normal and find the paranormal…
The mystic marriage…yet it is so practical…

April 22, 2001 at Lake Siskiyou, Mount Shasta, California

The Wordless and Nameless

There is a Wordless and Nameless Presence that humanity names. Endless names we pin upon this invisible formless Presence that pervades all things. This Presence that is everywhere Present is not only named but fought about unmercifully by people of the world. The people of the world fight about how we acknowledge IT in our lives. The traditions, religious, spiritual groups, nations, tribes all speak about IT by different names, customs, rituals, ceremonies, and non-ceremonies.

IT is called Spirit, God, Great Mystery, the Sacred Now, the One Self, Love, Christ, the Presence, Essence, Holy Presence, Father, the Great Mother, Source, Principle, The Holy One, The Holy of Holies, Truth, the Power, Energy, Life, Holy Ghost, Oneness, the Light, the All that IS, what IS, Isness, I, I am, I Am That, the One Life, Goddess, Consciousness, and endless other names around the world.

And IT, this wordless and nameless presence, is worshipped, celebrated, prayed to, preyed to, invoked, danced to, sung to. In all of the gesturing and posturing in relationship to this Presence, there may be a tendency to get attached to the form of devotion and move into a sense of separation from the IT.

This Presence is everywhere present. It lives through us and as us. It is the one as the many, Creator as creation. As! As is a very special and important word in our understanding, for it "eliminates" the sense of separation.

One may sit quietly and ponder and reflect on "the Presence" AS the I of anything.

And all changes. An essence is felt…a holy Presence. And one begins to realize that just as Life flows through a seed to make it a bud and then a beautiful flower, so too does that same Life flow through us and all other forms and non forms.

Then comes the precious Realization that the Life that flows through Nature, flows through us. There is but One Life.

And as we harmonize and align our heart, mind, and soul with that One Life, we harmonize with all Life. And harmony is felt.

We came upon this globe to experience the one as the many, the many as the one. Never were we meant to experience the fear, pain, suffering of separation. Let us get this "story of Oneness" in our Consciousness. For Consciousness is who we are.

The true story of humanity is the constant celebration of this Oneness. Let us not buy the lies, the false stories in the marketplace of human life, that we were intended to be in this human misery. The human pain is just a guidepost that we are missing the boat, so to speak. It does not mean to cope with it, manage it, embrace it. Realize simply that one is not in the Oneness.

Begin to find the openings, the portals into this Presence. It is a wordless, nameless, timeless state of Consciousness. And it is everywhere present. It already is. Only our human consciousness must return to IT, to enjoy the wonders, the ecstasy and the ceaseless exaltations. It is the rapture of the ages. And it is experienced as Consciousness…and a celebration of the Oneness…

May 24, 2001

The Holy Presence of Love

The Holy Presence of Love
is before you, behind you, above you, below you.
It is everywhere. It is abundant.
And it is yours.

It beckons from behind the scenes of man's imaginings.
It beckons.

It awaits.
It awaits your holy sight.
It awaits your holy hearing.

It changes all things in a twinkling.
All manner of thought turns to dust,
and borne is the pounding of love that fills your heart…

And you do see that it fills all Life…
for this holy presence of love is Life
and it is everywhere…

*I come from nowhere
and I go nowhere…
and I am everywhere…*

*You seek me only on dark nights
between the sheets and between your legs…
yet I tell you…I am everywhere…*

*Begin to see me thus…
For I am everywhere…*

*You dream I lie hidden only in another's heart
when I am everywhere...
You dream that you need to find me
when I am everywhere...*

*You cry silently in the night
because you cannot find me...
yet I am everywhere...*

*I say...
find me in the beating of your heart...
Feel my presence there...
Get very still...
that the clamor of the world falls into silence...
Let it die away...*

*And there I am...
From here...you feel no need to rush around...
to hurry here and there...*

*Litany fills your ears...
and you sleep and dream...
I call you now to wake...*

*I am in your breast, I say...
and I am everywhere...*

December 13, 2001 at 3 a.m. in Mount Shasta, California

True Power

It is 5:45 a.m. and this thought does come…

The people of Atlantis, we are told, misused the power, misused the crystals…

Then comes the thought…

If you have really gone deep enough within, and touched the God within, the Power within, then the Power of God uses you. You do not use the Power. The Power of God is Love. It cannot be misused. It is the life force that uses you. Expresses through you. You are only an instrument, a vessel, a nothingness, through which this Power does live.

The misunderstanding of true Power is what causes the belief in the misuse of power, be it in Atlantis or be it in the world as you know it today. And including the male and female power.

Let us gather in a new understanding. Let us perceive true Power, with a capital P, as the life force of that which we know as love. Love, dear ones, cannot be misused.

Love can only be "cast upon the waters" and it will return to you as love. Give and you shall receive. That is love. Allow that love and life will bloom.

It is missed in its utter simplicity. It is covered by economics, statistics, predictions, projections, graphs, and charts. All of those are the mortal mind trying to figure it out on the physical level. It can never be figured out from that level. Never.

For it is the outpouring of Spirit, of Presence. And it cannot be measured. It is the infinitude of being and it will pour forth as you allow the Love to flow forth.

Allow love to have a form.

When you seem to lie fallow in a moment of Earth time, you are both disconnecting from human figurings that bring naught and you are gathering in the awareness of this love. This presence of love is who you are. Let it flow…let it flow…

Begin just where you are to let it flow. No matter how simple, how misunderstood, how unrecognized. Let it flow. It will find a resting place and love will return to you.

Remember, love cannot be misused. It only flows forth and uplifts all in its current.

January 18, 2002 at 5:45 a.m. in Mount Shasta, California

Got Problems?

When you appear to have a problem, what can you do?
You may go where there are no problems.

A place where there are no problems?
It is not a place…it is a state of Consciousness,
an awareness of Presence…

There is only a vast Isness that can be felt and experienced. And It can animate us with even no question. And if, anyway, we ask a question and we go into the Consciousness of Presence, we shall find that our mind translates what we then view as an answer.

It is a splendid alchemy. It is a clear awareness of Consciousness unfolding. It is the highest quantum physics acted out in the most simple, ordinary acts of our lives. It is precious. It is "chop wood, carry water." It is the foundation from which smiles shall beam from the faces of the world.

We are of the heaven world, while we act as if we are trapped in hell, when it is, that we are only trapped in the false concepts of the ever human mind. Let us together leave this seeming realm of separation. Let us experience the alchemy in every situation.

And the problems…they do disappear…

May 12, 2002 at 9:27 a.m.
while driving to the East Bay, California

There Is No Shadow

Ever in the human mind is there a strong clinging belief in good and evil, light and dark.

And ever is there a determination that dark is evil, instead of a polarity of light in this world of opposites.

However, the apparent shadow known as human evil is merely a belief, usually a false human belief, a mere thought held tenaciously as true in the human mind.

Many there are who are battling and fighting these corpses; they seem content with the belief of their need to struggle with this shadow self.

The shadow self only exists from the place of separation from Source. At least the seeming sense of separation.

With the release of the finite sense of self, that shadow is no more. It disappears as the sun comes up.

The appearance of what is being described as a shadow self is merely the light of our own being touching a false concept in the mind. It then emerges as a human trait, such as anger, hatred, selfishness, and resentment.

Should we desire to leave the mystery or fascination of the shadow world, we can not only walk toward the light, but we find ourselves revealed as the Light. It is in this way that shadows (concepts/beliefs) are exposed by the light. We may allow them to surface and disappear.

If, when they surface, we entertain them, indulge in them, or get lost analyzing them, then we shall perpetuate the shadow and nourish and feed it. Sometimes we are proud of them or comfortable and familiar with them. They are character traits that feel like old friends and we hesitate to let them go. Perhaps we then think, at least we are somebody, even if it is the "black hat."

The truth is…we are nobody. We are light manifest as a form to animate. Should we make a transparency of our own mind, the shadow shall be no more.

We shall ask, "Where has the shadow gone? Who am I now?" It is at that moment, in this openness of consciousness, that we begin to allow our lives to emerge…the fullness and truth of our lives.

If we continue to push around the illusory world of effects, that is the 3D world of visible form, just that long shall we sustain being confused and confounded. There are actually people in the world who profit by our being and staying confused and confounded.

We must consciously choose to leave this world of human miscreation, the beliefs in good and bad.

We must, with awareness, enter this state of consciousness…
Presence Is.
And shadows…
they never were…
And begins…
a new day…

December 15, 2003 while driving I-5
from Los Angeles to San Francisco

I Desire ONLY Presence: Prayers or Preyers...

Now why would one desire only Presence? There are so many endless things in this created world to desire. And day after day, humanly our list grows and changes and often bulges.

We pray/prey to Spirit for this and that. We supplicate, we beg, we pray endless prayers and formulas and affirmations. We do ceremonies and rituals. Our desires deepen. We picture, we visualize, we outline long lists to the Infinite.

And in that we erect barriers; we erect Berlin Walls to our own joy and happiness. We perpetuate our longing and our yearning reaches great proportions.

Might we create these endless lists, using these prayers? Yes, we can create it all humanly...with effort, struggle, and trying.

And yet our prayers have made of us preyers?

Let us return to the true prayer that is a deep contact... communion...a union with Presence...with the Infinite... with the very substance of creation.

> And in that union, fulfillment happens.
> That which we need arrives.
> The void is filled.

And how is it that we erect a barrier in the very human desire for a material thing in the external world?

We erect a barrier thus. To humanly desire a person, thing, or place, we have to presume the lack of it. When we presume a lack, we create and perpetuate the lack.

    Fulfillment is ours. It is already ours.

Should any of us momentarily go out of balance and get sick by any name, we immediately wish for, desire for, that sickness, that disease to disappear. We must picture our lack of wholeness to picture the leaving of the disease.

    In that…we erect often a barrier of steel.
    In that…we perpetuate the seeming human problem.
    In that…we are in the human world of miscreation
    and digging, often deeper.
    In that…we are in human lack of Wholeness.
    And in that…we have forgotten our True Identity.

    Friends…we are that wholeness…
    we are that fulfillment…
    we already are…

    And it is not in a faraway world.
    It is not in a special formula or prayer.
    It is not in the seeming power of human desire.

    It…the fulfillment…this wholeness we seek…
    It lies within our heart.
    It lies within our soul.
    And…It…awaits our seeing.
    It…awaits…our coming home.

    And that home…it is within.
    Within our body? No…
    Within our Infinite Consciousness.

Come Home…I say…
Come Home…to your Infinite Consciousness…

There is no faraway God to pray/prey to.
There is no God out in the sky.
There is only Consciousness.
Consciousness is the God you seek.

And…friends…you are that Consciousness.

This Consciousness that you must Desire…
is your very own Awareness.
It is a storehouse of creation.
It is the substance of creation.
It is Grace.
All you could ever want, need, desire…
pours forth from this Infinite Substance.

Why does it not seem or appear that this is so? For we are blocking our own fulfillment in painful longing for endless things in the external world.

Let us end this parade of obstacles.
Let us end the human suffering borne of desire.
Let us enter the profound awareness of
…I have…
…I Already have…
Thank you God; I Already have…
Feel it as so.

Let us come into this radical knowing, this depth of understanding, of this principle, this universal principle of abundance through the simple awareness of…
Thank you God…
I Already have…

And feel this as so, for this is not a mental exercise nor an affirmation. Rather is this a state of consciousness to be attained.

O how difficult is this for which I speak, when the opposite seems so.

The world of human desire is the order of the day. Humanity thrives on the desires, borne of lack consciousness. Lack is different than the Emptiness that we find deep within…our very own Consciousness.

There it is that the paradox arises.
In the Emptiness that is the Fullness…the fulfillment is found.

There is found…that which we have been seeking.
There…within…it is found.

And it comes…
In our outer world…it does come…
By touching the substance of creation…it comes…
It is the Aladdin's Lamp…
It is the mystical made practical…
It does appear to be magic…

And…friends…it is grace…
This grace does pour into our lives…
And we do smile…
In fulfillment…we do smile…

No longer do we need to run around wanting, needing, desiring, lacking.

No longer do we have to figure out with our clever scheming human minds how to "get."

No longer do we have to struggle with the human concept of "I am without."

Friends…it is a concept. It is a misunderstanding of the law. It is a bypassing of Universal Principle…that sits within our reach.

It is like having a bank account filled with all our desires and not knowing how to open it. We have not known of it, nor had the key to open it.

We open it thus.

We open it with contact, union with Consciousness. This Consciousness is God, by whatever name we choose. Actually, we don't even open it. It has always been open.

> We allow it with "awareness of what Is…what Already Is."
> We allow it to flow.
>
> Abundance happens…
> and barrenness ceases to be…
>
> Friends…we are chasing ghosts…
> Even if we do catch a something in this world…
> it is fleeting…
> In a moment…it can cease to be…
>
> Let us catch a glimpse of the vision of the Infinite…
> In that…there is fulfillment…
> and pain of yearning…it does cease…

At the place where we make contact with Presence…we break the seeming separation between the inner/outer world.

At that place is the sacred spot of mystical union, mystical marriage.

At that place does our good begin to flow into what appears to be our outer life.

Friends…be in that union.

There it is that we drop human control.
There it is that we do not use mental might.
There it is that we shift from trying to use the Light…
to allowing It to use us…
There it is that struggle falls away.

In that union…the unknown becomes the known…

Supply can flow to us from the Infinite in ways that the mind cannot imagine or even conceive. That supply can arrive in magical ways or so ordinary and mundane as almost to be missed. So simple is this flow of abundance and supply into our existence.

Then it is that this supply may flow from us…as the giving. In the giving is the regiving and…Infinite supply is at hand.

March 16, 2004 at 1 a.m. in Taos, New Mexico

You Have Won the Lottery

What is it you hear from the mouths of so many?
"I would like to win the lottery."

Friends, I tell you.
You have won the lottery.
You have. I have. We all have.
You have won God's Lottery.
You have been chosen.
You have always been chosen.

It is only that you have forgotten.
How can you collect if you have forgotten?

You think thus. I have not.
And so it is that…you have not.

We claim that condition that is appearing and seems to be seen in the appearance world. We thus perpetuate that condition.

Strange, we perpetuate that human miscreation, when the opposite is true.

The truth is…I have.
The truth is…I already have.
Not tomorrow or next week…
but…Already…
The lottery that is ours is an inheritance…
We hear so much about getting rich by inheritance…

Well, each of us is now informed of an inheritance. Only we can claim it. Only we can live it. No one can do it for us. Wielding power in the external world will not do it.

Only acknowledging the only Power in the universe can claim it. Only making contact with that Presence will bring it forth in the outer world…that is the appearance world we call our lives.

To collect our lottery, our inheritance, we must on a day to day basis come in contact with this Presence. Thus it is that our effects world, our appearance world, begins to change.

Touching Presence, that is, the Cause, the Invisible, brings forth the "effects" world, into the visible and the physical.

It is not a working or struggling, a trying, a visualizing. It is not even dreaming. It is an allowing for the demonstration of Presence and staying with that.

It is grace.
Friends, it is grace.
It is the flowing forth…
and it is yours.
It is mine.
It is the world's.

Why are not millions collecting this inheritance,
that is the God Lottery?

Most people do not even know that this is so.
And if they heard that this is true, would they even open to it?

Some might say, "Wow, what a great belief."
Friends, this is not a belief.
This is the gift.
It is how it is.
It is universal law…principle.
It is the fulfillment.

Is there a price to pay? Not exactly. There is a Consciousness to attain. It is thus.

I have.
I Already have.
Thank you God, I Already have.

Feel that as so.

This is not a mantram or an affirmation to be endlessly repeated. This is the simple truth. It is attained in Consciousness…one person at a time.

It is not easy to attain, for the opposite seems true. One's life or others' may seem to be greatly lacking in endless lists of things.

Friends, enter into this Presence.
It is the very substance of creation
and it will begin to draw unto you that which is already yours.
For it is your inheritance.
It is your bank.
It is your storehouse.

Receive it.
Go into the Silence
and attain the sweet awareness,
the sweet consciousness of…
I have.
I Already have.
Thank you God, I Already have.
And feel that this is so.

Leave forever the consciousness of lack.
Leave forever the consciousness of "I don't have."
Leave forever the consciousness of limitation.

By opening to this Presence,
you inherit all.
You inherit all that God has.

By opening to this Presence in your inner life,
you open to a flow in your outer life.
And the separation is but a seeming.

That flow is a river.
A river of life…
and it does flow…

Let us not dam/damn this flow with endless curses and spells on our lives of "I don't have." When that flow begins to come… receive it from the Infinite…feel gratitude…and begin to give…

Give…
It is in the giving…that we are regiven.

Begin this day.

Realize in Consciousness…divine inheritance.
It is grace.
Grace is the true state.

Let us begin.

When the collective begins to "get it," to understand it, and most important, to apply and practice this law, we will witness a rapid quickening. People everywhere will begin to "get it."

Rivers of tears will flow.
Not tears of sadness…
but tears of relief and appreciation…

And humanity shall begin a new day. This day will grow into the next day and the next and it will be seen collectively that we are entering a new world. One person at a time.

That world is not even new. It has ever been awaiting in our Consciousness…

So busy we have been with battling, struggling, surviving in this foreign hostile world of duality where the opposites do seem to fight.

> *There is no battle. It is only a seeming.*
> *That battle is left by going into Presence.*
> *In Presence, there is no battle.*
> *In Presence, there is no opposition.*
> *God has no opponent.*
>
> *Peace is.*
> *Abundance flows.*
>
> *And grace…it is ours.*
>
> *Open this day…*
> *Receive…*

At first, this practice of "thank you God, I Already have" may seem foreign, awkward, and perhaps even untrue since the opposite certainly seems true. But after a while something begins to happen.

> *One begins to "feel" the knowingness of "I have."*
> *Joy begins to surface in one's Consciousness.*
> *Ecstasy, even, does find its rightful place.*

And dance begins to come.
True life is a dance.
It is the One Dance.

Equal giving and regiving is this dance.
It is love in motion and mutual reciprocity.
And joy…it does come.
It does dance across one's face.
Faces everywhere begin to smile.

We are that smile.
That smile does herald the emerging world…
that lies within our consciousness.

March 21, 2004 at 1:45 a.m. in Taos, New Mexico

Experience God

Many people are trying to get healings, money, homes, and mates…all without realizing that this is a focusing on the external material world of effects…a material manifestation.

Should we shift that focus to the Holy Presence, that is everywhere present, we will discover that all of those material things are the "added things" that come as a seeming miracle.

We will discover that this Presence is the Wholeness that we are looking for. We will discover that this Presence is the home, the transportation, the partner, the good health, the supply that we have been looking for. Even…it is…that we have been searching for, struggling for and striving for.

Let us end this futile struggle, this mad scramble for the material universe. Do not mistake these things for happiness and joy. And paradoxically, we may have them all. But they are not the focus, the goal, the demonstration.

The desire here is for only the experience of God…of Presence. This experience alone allows another world to emerge from inside one's Being.

These words I speak are not to be confused with religion. To enter into the consciousness, the lucid awareness of the Presence of God and thus allow "another world" is a universal law. It is a principle; it is true science. It was here before religions and traditions.

And it can only be proved in the living of it. The living of it demands the understanding of the principle, the consciousness of it. And it demands the practicing of it.

And it demands the seeing that this is available for all. Not a few, not a select chosen few, but for all who awaken to it and practice.

In the realization of this law, we are free. We are no longer in bondage to the theories and false beliefs and superstitions. We are free. And we extend this awareness to others as they are in readiness.

Such joy shall be ours…
as we give this gift…
Such freedom we have never known…
as now does live our lives…

Let us be in gratitude, not just for the exaltation of our own expanded awareness.

Let us be in gratitude that this is so for All. That All includes the kingdoms and the elements…and even the seeming enemy.

All…
That All is us…
We are One…

May 9, 2004 at 2:30 a.m. in Taos, New Mexico

The Promise

History has been the demonstration of the lack of balance.

Each battle of the polarities has been a fortifying of this imbalance. Each movement into matriarchy or patriarchy has been a fortifying of this imbalance.

Endless stories of this recorded imbalance fill our libraries, movies, curriculums, and our hearts and minds.

Such lack of cultural equilibrium has played out, is playing out, and will be playing out until the collective does awaken to learn, know, and live this Law of Balance which is Love's Dance upon the Earth. Equilibrium in all of Nature does reign as the principle of peace. And humanity must see.

Lost we have been in the annals of history, recording in space our misfortunes borne of misery and ignorance of the law.

Ever shall we find more misery in thoughts and actions of imbalance.

And long shall be our days and long our nights should we continue in this saga of sin borne of separation from Balance. And long shall be our pain.

Who would tell you that suffering is your teacher…
leads you into the land of the blind.

Nevermore sit in these woes as if they were your latest idol
upon the throne of untruth.

Nevermore place them on a pedestal
to build strong your self-inflicted misery and self-pity.

Another teacher awaits.
It lies, not within your body; it lies deep within your Being,
as Consciousness, as awareness.
And should you enter your Consciousness deeply enough,
you shall find the pearl of Knowing.

You shall end the ceaseless prayers and lamentations of not knowing.
You shall find your consciousness is Consciousness,
with no separation.
You shall find that which you call Love.
You shall find that which you do call Peace.
You shall find that which you call Freedom.
And you shall find that which the world calls supply
in this grand world of effects,
that is our garden, our playground of ecstasy.

And your days shall be filled
and your nights…
Time and space shall be filled
with endless melody…
It is all here…in Consciousness…
That Consciousness…Already Is…
Enter now…the "land of IS"…
Enter now…a realm of unending pleasure…
not human pleasure that versus pain…
But the pleasure of the Infinite…
bestowing upon you…your Life…

May 20. 2004 while driving from Taos to Albuquerque

Respond to Inner Vision

*Let us each respond to inner Vision,
rather than react to the outer world of miscreations
borne of human false concepts and the battle of duality....*

It is often very difficult to not be swept up in the "outer seeming of the appearance world." I say unto you that...the world is within. There is nothing but Consciousness in all the Universe. Whether we stay in and "react" to the outer human consciousness of the battle of duality of the ever human scene, that is of the finite sense, is up to us.

Until each and every one of us goes ever deeper, we will be living "in reaction" to what appears to be human power given always to someone or something external. Sometimes it is feeling victim to a political party with its beliefs. Tomorrow it will be something else. This is all a human state of misidentification and feeling the pain of that misidentification.

There is only One Power and it is the Power of the Infinite. Each of us that goes within and allows that One Power to give us vision can go into action Now. Each precious soul has a Vision to be Lived in Action...Now. The Mystical as the Practical... Now. The outer turmoils change one thing...the desire in each to go ever deeper within into the Realm of the Real. Feel the ecstasy of the realm of the real.

There is much more Light/Consciousness on the planet than ever before. That light shines through those who open to the light. We are that very light. We can only allow it to live through us as love, wisdom, and all the other supreme qualities. With more Light, those thoughts and actions that break the universal

Law of Balance, the law of love, do surface to be released. We cannot waver when those things that break the Law of Love do surface to be released. It is good. They are exposed. We must see them in the light of love. We must give them holy sight.

This is not a time to give power to duality of parties, duality of genders, duality of anything. The One Power knows no opposites. It is one. Duality is the realm of endless and painful battle of opposition and karma, devoid of grace.

Let us be empowered by the Vision of the One Power.

Let us allow this Consciousness to reveal to us our script, our actions, our expressions and responses of the supreme creativity, this supreme love and wisdom, which married…bears beauty.

This is not a time to "outline" to the Supreme Consciousness what we want and cry like children if we do not get it. This is a time to allow that Consciousness of Oneness to live in us, through us, around us, and as us.

This is not a time to give power to the finite universe. This is a time to quit externalizing power and authority, whether in government or in spiritual matters. This is a time to finally be in that lifetime, that one finds revealed within the Self… "direct knowing."

Awa Tey Ewa Tey. Now is the time.

Direct knowing, friends. It is a time for direct knowing. Any one of us could turn the tides, for "the within IS the without," the "as above IS the below." There is no separation. Listen within, like never before, and do what is ours to do in this beautiful and precious "play of creation." Do not believe that breaking the inviolate and inexorable Law of Love has any power. The Power is within.

Allow it to live though us. We are the precious vessels of Infinity. We must not then act like victims of the "outer seeming!" Let us take responsibility for being the birthers of new forms... birthers of a new culture. The ancient meaning of culture is... "gathering of light." It really does not matter who is president for us to do this.

> We are the higher Consciousness unfolding.
> Let us be aware and do this now. It is time.

There is a growing multitude that has opened to the "light of knowing." Let that Light of Knowing be the direct revelation of our every moment. Let us live in the ecstasy of that Knowing, not in the false identification with and reaction to the outer world. This is our moment to know that Reality is within and that we are the instruments through which it manifests and materializes in the physical universe.

> Let us be the example of that.
> Each moment...let us radiate that knowing...

Let us not need or expect others to "change" the world.

Each Consciousness of each human that aligns with the One Mind, the One Power...will know what is his/hers to do. Let us begin this day...to leave "reaction to the outer world"...and let us respond to the Vision given to us from the One Self, our True Self, from within...

> Choose this day...to act or react...

2004 in Taos, New Mexico

A Child of Forever

It has happened. I am here. By human definition of age, I am aged. The world is full of thoughts about people that are aged and more. They are often disquieted by us.

And the truth is, I am young. I am free. I am freer than I have ever been. I am free of the rules. The endless rules. I am free of being careful of what to say. I am free of caring what others think.

> O…the child in me soars.
> The dreamer in me has no blocks.
> O…I do soar into the future in dreams.

What fun it is! Last night, in dream, I sat in a class in seeming "future time." We learned first about antigravity and began to move upward in space. I began first to levitate. All the rest of the class had been there before. All ages were there. This was not a matter of human concept of age.

Once I got the hang of it, I could lean back and then propel myself. I was soon soaring. I was soaring through the building.

There was nothing pulling me earthward. I was fully free. I was a bird…soaring in space.

No thoughts did clog my mind. No emotions held me back. Attachments to the Earth…there were none…Free…I tell you… Free…

Time did not dare pull me out of the sky. Time did not dare to be my master telling me when to do this and that.

No one dare tell me time is the Master and I should discipline myself to time. What a feigned life…time demands and portrays.

How many people are lined up at any counter or with surgeons trying to "buy freedom from time?"

How many do you see moving in that direction?

O…I say…I choose the timeless realm. Know that here there is no age. One is as a child of forever. Here one sees the human mind has been numbed by time. Freezing it. Time does freeze the mind in time and space. It is a prison. It is a prison…I say.

Flying is a timeless act.

O…the dream did come and show another world. The dream did show a world of no tomorrows. The dream did show the world of our seeming future. I did travel there…for I am ageless now…

In this future world that we wait for in the world of time, we are free. We all are free.

Cars. There are none.
And trucks. None.
Or busses.
There are none, I say.
There are none.

We fly.
We fly through the sky.
We are free.
Our body acts with jet propulsion.
It is all done in consciousness.

We don't remember how.
For our minds are filled with fear.
Fear of most everything does grip the mind.

We have created a world of fear.
And we are frozen in fear.
People grow slower…more catatonic by the day.

It need not be.
Our minds may be swept clean.
They may be transparent…
receiving only light…

Fed by the light, we can be…
should we care to change the menu…
It is we who choose the diet of fear
and we know it not…

We live with glimpses of some sought for freedom in retirement one day when we are exhausted of even being here.

"After I gain my fame and fortune," we say. "Or after the children are grown. Or even after the grandchildren."

We push freedom far into the future and it does die, weeping in the cage of mind.

O…I say…
We can have that freedom now.
We can be ageless in the mind.
And we can soar.

Freedom do we taste.
There is no stopping us.

I don now new clothes.
I cast away that which would limit me…
that which is sewn for those in time…
Restrictions have I done.

And joy does fill my heart…

June 5, 2004 at 3:30 a.m. in Taos, New Mexico

I have chosen to include this description of a lucid dream as a reminder that dreams may also give us "messages from the silence."

Presence Is...

Humanity has created many barriers and obstacles to awareness of Presence. Some of these barriers are false human concepts, judgments, condemnations (unholy sight), human desires, and drugs that block the flow. Beneath these layers of human thoughts, Presence Is...Presence Already Is...

Humanity must be prepared to and willing to release those human thoughts that block awareness. Presence never goes anywhere. It is everywhere. It is ever present...just awaiting our awareness.

It is a momentous event when we have even a glimpse into Reality and feel the love that we are and receive the wisdom that we are. This love...wisdom...is Consciousness and it does beckon. This love/wisdom is One in our heart. Love and wisdom are married in our heart and their expression into the world is unprecedented Beauty.

Humanity must empty of these barriers if it wants to depart from the drama of duality that brings endless suffering.

Theories, postulates, dogma are all barriers to Presence.

Get simple...like the children...feeling, listening, being. There is nothing to debate or argue. Simply...the practice of Presence.

February 2, 2005 in Taos, New Mexico

True Sustainability

The changes that we would like to see in the care of the world will not come in battle.

The changes we would like to see will come in leaving the battle.

The changes we would like to see will come through changing our consciousness.

The changes we would like to see will come through vision.

And the changes we would like to see will come by the simple living of that vision and the grounding of that vision.

Let us remember. There is only consciousness. There is only one Power…and true vision comes from that Power. True vision has no opposite.

Leave the battle.
And leave the world of prophecies and fears.

All prophesies and predictions are subject to change.

All prophesies and predictions are simply warnings, messengers of change.

Be that change.

Be that change borne of vision…not vision borne of fear or reason and never ending interpretations of the mind…but vision borne of the nameless One…vision borne of the Infinite.

Be that very change.

Should we enter the battle, we shall be mere puppets on the stage of duality, in the battle on a screen of never ending opposition. We shall be a force that perpetuates the battle. We shall enliven the battle. We shall use our consciousness to empower it and enflame it, as we have done all down through the ages in endless moments of fear.

Now should we leave the battle…there shall be no opposition. There shall be no fight. There shall be only the living of the vision. Only living of the power borne from in our hearts.

We can begin this shift.
We can begin this change of consciousness.

Together…we can live this vision…
Together…we can re-create the garden and more…
Together…we can do this…

We can do it in unison…
in unity…
We can create the greatest unification the world has ever known.

This vision borne of the heart will sustain itself.
This is the source of true sustainability.

Give no power to the external world.
Give no power to the old order.
It crumbles and falls.
It is not created with true vision.
It then has nothing, but us, the people,
to maintain and sustain it.

Withdraw attention. And build the new world.
It awaits our seeing. It awaits our sight.

Many are frightened.
We shall not find vision in fright.
Leave the world of fear and no tomorrows.
Leave it now.

It serves no purpose in what is ahead.
Together...we create a shift...
Together...we create an unprecedented shift...

History shall no longer hang its head and weep...
when the beauty of this new world does emerge
from the slumbering of a people with no vision...

February 17, 2005 at 2 a.m. in Taos, New Mexico

Mary Saint-Marie: Artist/Writer

Mary Saint-Marie is a mystic artist/writer/poet, spiritual educator, and visionary. Although *Messages from the Silence* follows three other books by Mary, this book came to her from the Silence over a period of years for the purpose of inspiring others into the Silence.

Mary has also birthed two recordings with the theme of Return to Oneness that are available. She has traveled nationwide exhibiting visionary art in over 150 shows.

Simultaneously, Mary has shared Soul Sessions, Soul Retreats, and multi-media Sacred Enactments of Ancient Remembering, called *SHE…It Is…Who Remembers,* inspiring others into the awareness of Oneness, the Presence, that each may express their true essence. She describes the work as The Mystical as Practical…Galactic Shamanism.

The mystical, sacred, and visionary paintings of Mary Saint-Marie are inspirational and mirror our Oneness with Creator/Creation. The sacred images are a reflection of the marriage of earth and sky, the yin and yang of our nature. They are a journey into the land of Archetypal Realms of Wholeness. They are witness to the Law of Balance, that is the universal and inviolate law of love. They speak to the direct knowing of I Am the Light of Being.

The paintings are multi-media and multi-technique and multi-dimensional. The unusual techniques used have come to Mary in the Silence. In addition, Mary has created many sculptures, revealing Life AS Living Ceremony.

Mary's paintings/work are found in *One Source Sacred Journeys, Songs from the Edge of Everything,* and *The Ways of Spirit.* Mary's art is also found on the covers of her previous books, *Galactic Shamanism, The Holy Sight,* and *Nectar of Woman.* The art has appeared on cards, calendars, and magazines, such as *Quest, Mystic Pop,* and *Anemone* in Japan. It has been featured on television nationwide via many stations, including the Wisdom Channel. And her art has been televised across Germany.

Mary's Art-of-the-Soul is collected nationally and internationally.

Mary has been pioneering art exhibitions that reveal universal principles of Oneness since 1972 in galleries, conferences, symposiums, expositions, faires, and workshops.

* Mary Saint-Marie's books *Galactic Shamanism* and *The Holy Sight* describe Mary's awakening into the Soul Realm of Light in 1971. They also describe the ensuing journeys during the 80's and 90's into the Archetypal Realms of HE and SHE, during meditation, revealing the Life of Oneness wanting to be lived upon this plane of existence, through man and woman.

Archetypal teachings and Lemurian mergings with Nature were revealed via archetypes, such as Changing Woman, Spider Woman, White Buffalo Woman, and the Blue Kachinas. Mary was uplifted in consciousness repeatedly into the Christed realm of the animals and given revelations of how they await humanity's coming.

In 1981, Mary experienced a nine hour meditation of expanding from ordinary consciousness to pure Consciousness. Pure I Am Awareness. Direct knowing beyond teachers and teachings. She experienced form and formless as one.

Mary inspires and initiates others through sessions, retreats, art, and writing to come into awareness of Essence and Oneness and leave the human sense of separation from the precious and Illumined Source.

Mystic Art, Books, Sessions, and Retreats

Mystic Art

Fine Art Giclee Reproductions are available. Inquire about original art.

Books

Books may be ordered on Amazon.

Galactic Shamanism
The Sacred Two
The Holy Sight
Nectar of Woman
Messages from the Silence
The Star-Stone Two
The Animating Presence
The Monitor and Laughter of the Gods
Art as Consciousness
The Oracle and the Dreamer

CDs

Soul Sounds of World Birth
Journey of Consciousness

Website gives more information about:
Mystic Art
Soul Sessions
Soul Retreats
Holy Sight workshops

Note the youtube videos and interviews.

www.marysaintmarie.com
www.EarthCareGlobalTV.com

www.ingramcontent.com/pod-product-compliance
Lightning Source LLC
Chambersburg PA
CBHW050647160426
43194CB00010B/1841